# EXERCISES for When Words Collide

## A Journalist's Guide to Grammar and Style

## Lauren Kessler
## Duncan McDonald

School of Journalism
University of Oregon

Wadsworth Publishing Company
Belmont, California
A Division of Wadsworth, Inc.

© 1985 by Wadsworth, Inc. All rights reserved. No part of this book may be reproduced, stored in a retrieval system, or transcribed, in any form or by any means, electronic, mechanical, photocopying, recording, or otherwise, without the prior written permission of the publisher, Wadsworth Publishing Company, Belmont, California 94002, a division of Wadsworth, Inc.

Printed in the United States of America

1 2 3 4 5 6 7 8 9 10 — 89 88 87 86 85

ISBN 0-534-02781-4

# Preface

In the preface to *When Words Collide* (*WWC*), we stress that language is a lifeline for all of us, not just for the professional communicator. Professional writers and editors, however, have an even greater dependence on the use of language. For them, weak grammar and poorly directed style have dire implications.

This exercise book builds on the foundation of the *WWC* text by providing a step-by-step program of learning and review of grammatical principles. The 33 exercises, which include two evaluative exams, closely follow the textbook's order of presentation. We urge you to complete all exercises; you will find that most of them can be completed in 20 minutes or less. When you have the opportunity to review the answers, refer to pertinent pages in *WWC* to reinforce key points. If possible, do the exercise again—or better yet, create some new questions and answer them!

We are convinced that the best way to build and maintain a good foundation in grammar is through careful arrangement of its building blocks. Our "blueprint" starts with parts of speech and proceeds through identifying and using sentence elements and identifying phrases and clauses; then we take up sentence construction, agreement, case, parallelism, voice, subordination and modification, word use, spelling, clarity and conciseness, and style. Style without grammatical foundation is like a sailboat without rudder or keel: It may occasionally exhibit dramatic moves, but it is doomed to misadventure.

Exercises 27 and 28 provide a good opportunity for testing all your grammatical skills by forcing you to edit for errors and unclear presentation. Exercises 29–32 test your oganization and clarity as they move you into the realm of journalistic writing.

If you closely follow the *WWC* text, this exercise book, the *Associated Press Stylebook* and your dictionary, you will improve your understanding and use of both grammar and style. With such a foundation—and the confidence it brings—your writing will move toward impressive horizons.

Our best wishes for endurance and enthusiasm!

L. Kessler
D. McDonald
Eugene, Oregon

# Contents

|  | Preface iii |
|---|---|
| EXERCISE 1 | Grammar and Spelling Pretest 1 |
| EXERCISE 2 | Parts of Speech 1 3 |
| EXERCISE 3 | Parts of Speech 2 7 |
| EXERCISE 4 | Parts of Speech 3 9 |
| EXERCISE 5 | Identification of Sentence Elements 11 |
| EXERCISE 6 | Identification of Phrases and Clauses 15 |
| EXERCISE 7 | Creation of Phrases and Clauses 19 |
| EXERCISE 8 | Strengthening Verbs 23 |
| EXERCISE 9 | Sentence Construction 1 25 |
| EXERCISE 10 | Sentence Construction 2 27 |
| EXERCISE 11 | Subject-Verb Agreement 31 |
| EXERCISE 12 | Antecedent Agreement 33 |
| EXERCISE 13 | That/Which/Who and Restrictive/Non-Restrictive Constructions 35 |
| EXERCISE 14 | Case 1 37 |
| EXERCISE 15 | Case 2 39 |
| EXERCISE 16 | Parallelism 41 |
| EXERCISE 17 | Proper Use of Voice 43 |
| EXERCISE 18 | Punctuation 1 47 |
| EXERCISE 19 | Punctuation 2 51 |
| EXERCISE 20 | Punctuation 3 53 |
| EXERCISE 21 | Subordination and Modification 55 |
| EXERCISE 22 | Word Use 1 57 |
| EXERCISE 23 | Word Use 2 59 |

EXERCISE 24   AP Style   63
EXERCISE 25   Spelling 1   65
EXERCISE 26   Spelling 2   67
EXERCISE 27   Editing for Grammar and Style   69
EXERCISE 28   Clarity and Conciseness   73
EXERCISE 29   Boiling 1   75
EXERCISE 30   Boiling 2   77
EXERCISE 31   Leads 1   79
EXERCISE 32   Leads 2   81
EXERCISE 33   Final Grammar, Spelling and Word-Use Exam   83

Name _____

Grade or score _____

# Strengthening verbs

EXERCISE 8

**Purpose**  To recognize and correct weak or imprecise verbs as a major step toward writing crisply and concisely.

**Reference**  *WWC*, pp. 11–15, 43, 114–116, 138

## PART ONE

**Instructions**  Sentences 1–10 suffer from weak verbs. The true action in a sentence may not be expressed in a straightforward construction that makes use of a strong verb. The verb may be hidden or overmodified. Determine the action (state of being, position) in each sentence. Reconstruct each sentence, aiming for strong, precise verbs.

**Example**  There was a speech by the senator on campus today. What action is stated or implied in this sentence? *Speaking* is the action. The sentence should be reconstructed to make use of a strong verb, for example: *The senator spoke on campus today.*

1. She said that German had been her minor in college.

2. They really worked very hard on the project.

3. There will be a march by the striking teachers tomorrow.

23

4. When I have arrived at the age of 80, I plan to be both healthy and wise.

5. It is the mayor's plan to run for re-election.

6. His voice was extremely loud and angry when he spoke to the class.

7. The committee members have been having arguments with each other.

8. It was the captain who gave the order to move forward to the troops.

9. The governor said she would look very carefully at the report and that she would personally conduct an investigation of the agency.

10. He could not make an identification of the killer from the police photographs.

## PART TWO

**Instructions**   Replace each of the following phrases with one strong, precise verb. Be careful not to change the meaning of the phrase.

11. hold tightly            _____
12. complain constantly     _____
13. eat quickly             _____
14. interrupt the progress of _____
15. imitate the actions of  _____
16. move forward slowly     _____
17. talk incessantly        _____
18. sleep lightly           _____
19. walk drunkenly          _____
20. take advantage of       _____

# Parallelism

**EXERCISE 16**

**Purpose**  To create grammatical consistency within sentences by learning to recognize and create parallelism in series, tense, voice and gender.

**Reference**  *WWC,* Chapter 4, especially pp. 58–65 and 128–131

**Instructions**  Some of the following sentences contain errors in parallelism (series, tense, voice and gender). Others are correct as written. Rewrite the incorrect sentences to ensure parallelism. Mark *C* for correct next to the sentences you feel do not need rewriting.

_____ 1. The council members faced two items on their agenda: a searching for the solution to the sewage treatment problem and figuring out a way to bring more high-tech jobs to the county.

_____ 2. She's a fine sailboat; however, she's difficult to maneuver occasionally and always a great expense.

__C__ 3. The candidate surveyed the audience, reviewed his notes and began his sixth speech in eight hours.

_____ 4. Her speech was strident but also had that quality that really uplifts.

41

_____ 5. The commission released its findings on the July slaying of Carrie Greenfield, but its report on the gambling ring was withheld.

_____ 6. One should never argue with an umpire; people should know that by now.

_____ 7. Your coat size is bigger than your older brother.

_____ 8. Everyone is entitled to his or her opinion.

_____ 9. Your habit of transcribing all your interview tapes and me constantly insisting on hiring two proofreaders will cause us to miss many deadlines and unlimited anxiety.

_____ 10. The council approved the zoning ordinance, but the assessment resolution was defeated by them.

_____ 11. A doctor does not always know what is best for his patients.

_____ 12. The mayor discussed next year's projection of revenues, new procedures for zoning variances and that the apartment vacancy rate is falling.

# Proper use of voice

**EXERCISE 17**

**Purpose**  To learn to write more forcefully and crisply by using active voice constructions, and to identify the occasional construction that is better served by passive voice.

**Reference**  *WWC*, Chapter 6

**Instructions**  The secret to using active voice is to make the *subject* of the sentence perform. Make the subject *act* rather than being *acted upon*. In the following passive voice sentences: (1) circle the agent that performs the action; (2) underline the object or receiver of the action; (3) rewrite the sentence in the active voice—unless passive voice is more effective in that particular example. However, if you make no change, explain your decision. Some items lack an agent or a recipient.

Example    The <u>match</u> was won by (Sugar Ray Leonard.)

        Sugar Ray Leonard won the match.

1. The <u>payments</u> were accepted by (the vice president.)

    *The vice president accepted the payments.*

2. There was thick <u>smoke</u> being dodged by (the firefighters.)

    *Firefighters dodged the thick smoke*

3. Former city councilor Tom Jewett was arrested last night for drunken driving.

4. Tons of deadly particles were carried by wind currents.

5. He is called a progressive in thin disguise by others.

6. The soggy cash was counted and dried by the sheriff.

7. Her decision was to sit in the corner until she was asked to dance.

8. At dusk, the whimpering of a wounded animal could be heard.

9. Every inch of space is claimed by bright toys.

*Bright toys claimed every inch of space.*

10. More than $3-million worth of negotiable bonds were stolen this morning by a man wearing a Captain Kangaroo costume at the First Interstate Bank.

11. There is a special defense measure that will be considered by the armed services committee.

12. The huge baskets of oysters were wrestled by French fishermen.

13. There were dead leaves covering the ground.

14. The football was thrown 85 yards from the quarterback to the split end.

15. At dawn, the crowing of a rooster was heard.

16. Allegations of impropriety were repeatedly denied by the press secretary.

17. An 85-year-old Middletown woman was killed by a hit-and-run vehicle last night.

18. Delegates were told by the UNESCO secretary-general that elimination of U.S. funding would cripple the organization.

19. There was a belching noise made by Cool Hand Luke.

20. The meeting was gaveled to order by Jennifer Miles.

Name _____

Grade or score _____

# EXERCISE 19

# Punctuation 2

**Purpose**   To learn how to use commas, colons and semicolons correctly.

**Reference**   *WWC*, Chapter 7

**Instructions**   Punctuate the following sentences with commas, colons and semicolons as appropriate. *Do not use* any other punctuation marks. Some sentences are correct; mark them *C*.

_____ 1. Present at the meeting were: Marcia Haller, state highway geologist; Larry Anderson, University of Oregon archeologist; and Richard Ramus, president of Citizens for Better Transportation.

_____ 2. Smith said, they'd "get rich quick;" Jones said, they'd "get dead quicker."

_____ 3. To the governor, all crises of the past three years added up to one major problem, lack of funds.

_____ 4. Susan Stamberg, anchor of "All Things Considered," flew to Boston to receive the award.

_____ 5. They had to move, the landlord refused to fix the defective chimney.

_____ 6. Benton county farmers, grow alfalfa, hops, grapes and mint.

_____ 7. Six people died during the October heat wave and four more were hospitalized in serious condition.

_____ 8. After a strenuous campaign that kept her on the road for five weeks the senator returned to Washington.

_____ 9. While the children were eating the mosquitos swarmed around the table.

_____ 10. Some of the Tylenol that was sold in Chicago drugstores was contaminated.

_____ 11. The sharp loud blast startled the onlookers.

_____ 12. The man who was waiting for the bus was drunk.

_____ 13. At 8:30 a.m. the students all wanted to do one thing sleep.

_____ 14. "But" she added "I'm never late."

_____ 15. The meteorologists say we'll have another soggy Northwest winter.

_____ 16. The week was hectic nevertheless the reporters met their deadlines.

_____ 17. The committee decided to postpone its discussion because the necessary documents were missing.

_____ 18. Smith himself will write the report.

# EXERCISE 21

# Subordination and modification

**Purpose**  To practice constructing crisp, readable sentences by correctly ordering, subordinating and modifying ideas.

**Reference**  *WWC,* pp. 26–27, 41–42, 122–128

**Instructions**  Edit the following sentences to eliminate oversubordination, split construction and misplaced or confusing modification. Rewrite if necessary.

1. Those who lie often are found out.

2. When she began her career, while only a teenager, Patsy Dant had trouble handling success.

3. While sprinting around the track, her long braids whipped in the wind.

4. Even after he landed the job, which seemed to fit his education and qualifications and which promised to make use of his special talents, he was still depressed.

5. City officials have promised for more than two years to replace the hazardous asbestos ceilings.

6. The newspaper story libeled Bob Carey, who was a congressman who then lost his bid for re-election.

7. The planning commission, after debating for two hours and hearing three hours of public testimony, vetoed the street-widening proposal.

8. If because his business calls for it he has to travel, he will.

9. She promised to as soon as she had time repair the leaky faucet.

10. After reading the newspaper in the bathtub, the ink was smudged all over his hands.

11. Because he needed the money, Nick took the bribe, although he knew he shouldn't.

12. Millworkers protested yesterday in front of Fircorp's plywood plant on the outskirts of Tipton a proposed cut in health benefits and overtime pay.

13. The women said that if they were drafted, they would serve their country on the battlefield or off.

14. The fraternity, by a 30-7 margin with four men refusing to vote, decided to ban smoking in the house.

15. People who eat fish frequently have low cholesterol levels in their blood.

# Word use 1

**EXERCISE 22**

**Purpose**  To add consistency and logic to writing by preserving the distinctive meaning of words.

**Reference**  *WWC*, Part Two, and *AP Stylebook*

**Instructions**  Make the correct word choice from the alternatives offered in the sentences.

_____ 1. *(a) Compared to (b) Compared with* last year's bumper crop, this year's corn yield per acre is pitiful.

_____ 2. Labor arbitrators should be *(a) disinterested (b) uninterested* parties in collective bargaining disputes.

_____ 3. Twelve *(a) people (b) persons* were killed in weekend accidents.

_____ 4. Potatoes *(a) that (b) which* are grown in Idaho have a national reputation for quality.

_____ 5. *(a) Because (b) Since* you failed to mail the warranty, the company will not honor your request for free repairs.

_a_ 6. *(a) Their (b) There* once-invincible stock portfolio is now the weakling of the Dow Jones playground.

_____ 7. What *(a) implication (b) inference* can you draw from his thinly veiled charges?

_a_ 8. It's only about six miles *(a) farther (b) further* to camp.

_a_ 9. The nuclear freeze demonstration attracted *(a) more than (b) over* 10,000 students.

_b_ 10. I don't believe that the plaintiff has *(a) proved (b) proven* his claim.

_b_ 11. The faculty senate *(a) censored (b) censured* the dean for her failure to produce a more convincing tenure package for the young professor.

_a_ 12. The baseball commissioner is convinced that the game needs *(a) fewer (b) less* free agents.

57

_____ 12. The baseball commissioner is convinced that the game needs *(a) fewer (b) less* free agents.

_____ 13. The candidate compared his opponent *(a) to (b) with* "a toad-sucking snake."

_____ 14. The party *(a) convinced (b) persuaded* her to run for the office.

_____ 15. The motor scooter *(a) crashed (b) collided* into the parked car.

_____ 16. In reading the prepared text of your speech, I sense that you are *(a) implying (b) inferring* that all military aid should be taken away from countries in violation of the treaty.

_____ 17. How do you explain his *(a) reluctance (b) reticence* to sign the contract?

_____ 18. The prisoner was *(a) hanged (b) hung* by the lynch mob.

_____ 19. How do you think this price rise will *(a) affect (b) effect* our sales projections?

_____ 20. The meeting will *(a) occur (b) take place* as scheduled.

_____ 21. *(a) Because of (b) Due to* the blizzardlike conditions at the Mount Hood pass, the ski team will delay its regular weekly conditioning trip.

_____ 22. This award-winning recipe is *(a) composed of (b) comprised of* seven "secret" ingredients.

_____ 23. She is *(a) anxious (b) eager* to present her findings to the committee.

_____ 24. You look *(a) as if (b) like* you've been watching too many political advertisements.

_____ 25. The candidate's staff was embarrassed that he *(a) alluded (b) eluded* to the controversial spending report.

Name _____

Grade or score _____

# EXERCISE 23

# Word use 2

**Purpose** To sharpen precision in word choice and to focus on the editing process to spot and correct word choice errors.

**Reference** *WWC,* Part Two, and *AP Stylebook*

**Instructions** Review the following sentences and correct all errors in word choice. Make corrections on these sheets with simple editing marks.

1. The speaker said she was not adverse to attempts to persuade her to change her position.

2. Set down and I'll recite the litany of all my broken principals.

3. This car's sticker price is under $5,000; compared to the cost of a new Excalibur, it's a real steal.

4. Since you are heading this committee, it is obvious that we will not examine this critical issue any farther.

5. Such complements from adoring fans have proven that underwater synthesized music is the future of rock and roll.

6. Over 300 persons composed the city's largest mass gathering against organic foods.

59

7. What was Bierce's quote about the American mass media?

8. Don't you realize that the affect of this news will sorely impact our earnings projections?

9. You can be sure that his speech meant to infer that the country is speeding towards double-digit inflation.

10. The work stoppage has effected fewer than three divisions of the company.

11. He has been persuaded to accept the agreement in principle.

12. She is anxious to present her findings on the charter amendment.

13. After he laid down for a while, he said he felt like he was a new man.

14. The economic summit will feature special negotiations among the World Bank, several Third World countries and three private financiers.

15. The senator's aid has repeatedly eluded to a "mysterious foreign force" on the finance subcommittee.

16. What is said to who with what affect?

17. Everyone is entitled to his opinion.

18. The winter hurricane ravished the North Carolina coastline.

19. The school principle reported that over 700 persons have applied for the position of teacher's aid.

20. Due to a failure of their own crops, Russia is expected to import a record amount of Western wheat this year.

21. The Argentine press did nothing to counter national euphoria with a more realistic view of a war which ultimately claimed the lives of hundreds of soldiers.

22. Are you persuaded yet of the correctness of my position?

23. The man spent the day just laying around his apartment.

24. I would compare his personality with the fresh, cool breeze of an early spring day.

25. Are you concerned that this recession will have a greater affect on the economy then last year's downturn?

# AP style | EXERCISE 24

**Purpose**  To become familiar with common journalistic style.

**Reference**  *AP Stylebook*

**Instructions**  Edit the following sentences, correcting all copy that does not conform to AP style.

1. Lieutenant Governor Eugene Lewelling, a member of the democratic party, testified today in Albany, NY before a special Congressional committee.

2. Prof. Ellen Williams, who has her bachelors degree from a small school in the northwest, is considered an expert on the supreme court's interpretation of the First amendment.

3. The drivers, members of the teamster's union, have asked for a pay increase of six per cent and for an 11% cost of living adjustment.

4. Representative Ann Black (R., Ohio) lives at Nine Baker Rd.

5. The UN will not comment on a report by the Federal Bureau of Investigation that an N.Y. diocese of the Episcopalian church is a cover organization for the communist party.

6. On Seattle's Skid Row, an unidentified man stole eight-year old Sandy Jenkin's seeing eye dog.

7. The inflation rate has climbed only .7% in the last eleven months, the President announced today.

8. Although she is only a 12th grade pupil at Saint Mary's school in Chico, CA., she is already making plans to earn a PHd degree.

9. 50,000 persons watched the $4,300,000 Baker-Schmentz bout.

10. The U.S. Post Office announced plans to increase the cost of sending a 1 oz. letter by two cents sometime during the next Fiscal Year.

11. The Nat. Organization of Women held its fifteenth rally in front of the Smithsonian Institute.

12. The Mississippi and Missouri Rivers are expected to crest at more than ten ft. above their flood stages before 10 p.m. this evening.

13. When questioned by the DA, police sergeant Bob Smythe testified at the Superior court trial that his Radar clocked the defendant's car at 82 m.p.h.

14. The cornbelt of Downstate Illinois has some of the most fertile land on this Continent.

15. The defendant, a retired Army Lt. Col., claimed he did not rob the jewels from the Ft. Lauderdale mansion of the A.B.C. executive.

Name

Grade or score

# Spelling 1 | EXERCISE 25

**Purpose**  To hone the vital skill of spelling.

**Reference**  WWC, Appendix A; Lewis, *Correct Spelling Made Easy*; your dictionary

**Instructions**  In each of the four-word sets below, choose the word that is spelled correctly.

| | | | | |
|---|---|---|---|---|
| ____ 1. | a. deterrant | b. weird | c. acceptible | d. cancelled |
| ____ 2. | a. changeable | b. advertizing | c. amoung | d. ocassion |
| ____ 3. | a. supercede | b. acommodate | c. copywright | d. compelled |
| ____ 4. | a. definate | b. couragous | c. tarrif | d. embarrass |
| ____ 5. | a. suprise | b. admissible | c. indispensible | d. annullment |
| ____ 6. | a. lonliness | b. alottment | c. appall | d. developement |
| ____ 7. | a. cemetary | b. priviledge | c. questionnaire | d. profitible |
| ____ 8. | a. parallel | b. persistant | c. withold | d. inferance |
| ____ 9. | a. caffiene | b. grammer | c. prefered | d. forcible |
| ____ 10. | a. licence | b. leisure | c. millionnaire | d. petulence |
| ____ 11. | a. macaber | b. profitted | c. noticeable | d. fullfill |
| ____ 12. | a. percieve | b. precede | c. temperment | d. resistent |
| ____ 13. | a. rivetted | b. tranquility | c. legitimit | d. pardonable |
| ____ 14. | a. proceed | b. kidnapping | c. practised | d. weild |
| ____ 15. | a. libelling | b. mathmatics | c. unanimous | d. maintainance |
| ____ 16. | a. neice | b. likible | c. vacillate | d. tendancy |

65

_____ 17. a. existance     b. dilemna       c. despicible    d. sovereign
_____ 18. a. atheletic     b. presumable    c. lothe         d. tresspass
_____ 19. a. ommit         b. broccoli      c. ossillate     d. manuver
_____ 20. a. newsstand     b. sieze         c. satilite      d. tryed
_____ 21. a. seperate      b. travelled     c. tonsillitis   d. recurrant
_____ 22. a. wellcome      b. vaccuum       c. villian       d. accidentally
_____ 23. a. abridgement   b. adolescent    c. rythm         d. alledged
_____ 24. a. benifit       b. cieling       c. descendant    d. distributer
_____ 25. a. chief         b. begger        c. donkies       d. dispair

Name _____

Grade or score _____

# Spelling 2

**EXERCISE 26**

**Purpose**  To continue to seek mastery of the skill of spelling.

**Reference**  *WWC*, Appendix A; Lewis, *Correct Spelling Made Easy*; your dictionary

**Instructions**  In each of the following sentences, one or more words may be spelled incorrectly. When you find an incorrectly spelled word, cross it out and write in the proper spelling. (In some sentences all words are spelled correctly.)

1. Her attorneys introduced documents coroborating the charge of sexual harrassment.

2. Conditions in the convalesent home were indescribable.

3. Although suseptible to occasional siezures of sloth, he is a suprisingly efficient worker.

4. The personable sophomore succumbed to skepticism.

5. The latest reconnissance mission yielded much relevent information about enemy forces.

6. His prounciation of certain words was noticably plebian.

7. The stationary was beautifully imbossed, but unfortunately the address was illegible.

8. He wanted to excell as a superviser, but the workers thought of him as a numbskull.

9. Her favorite pastime was correcting misspellings on posted notices.

67

10. The missellaneous merchandize includes twelve tins of tobbaco and forteen reversible jackets.

11. His predecessor, the sargent, had an outrageous temper.

12. Daily excercise is exhillarating, according to legions of amateur athletes.

13. The superintendant, known for her perserverance, had an irrepressible sense of humor.

14. He said the homemade mayonaise was completely indigestable.

15. The bookkeeper was besieged by a formidable array of tax auditors.

Name _____

Grade or score _____

# Editing for grammar and style

**EXERCISE 27**

**Purpose**  To incorporate all *WWC* readings and workbook exercises into a comprehensive editing exercise that tests grammatical principles.

**Reference**  *WWC* (all); *AP Stylebook*; Lewis, *Correct Spelling Made Easy*; your dictionary

**Instructions**  Review the following sentences and correct all errors in grammar, word use, AP style and spelling. Look carefully!

1. What the eyes see excite the brain.

2. What affect do you think this exam will have on we students?

3. Prof. William Jones inferred in his speech that supply-side economics will go the way of dinosoars.

4. The Porsche maneuvers quicker then the Lotus, it's torque-to-weight ratio is also more superior.

5. As I walked in to the police station I learned that a diner had robbed a fast food restaurant last night, because several persons at the establishment apparently offended him.

6. Compared to the three luxury yachts moared near-by the thirty-four-ft. sailboat look like it was a prize in a Cracker Jacks box.

7. 37-year-old Janet Springs died instantly this morning when the car which she was driving collided with a telephone poll.

8. The Jayhawk offense have proven they are a unit to reckon with; especially with their new use of Tom Clarke, who they stationed in a slot.

9. The condition of these buildings are disgraceful, nevertheless they shouldn't effect our ability to hold classes their.

10. The City Counsel will not hold it's regular monthly meeting, due to a power failure which hit the City Hall complex at five o'clock.

11. Whom did he say received the Congressional appointment?

12. If I was President of the United States, I'd be happy to solve this dillema, however, I'm not, and I just cant accomodate you. None of your arguments is going to convince me to change my mind.

13. The stockbrokers that signed the anti-trust petition discovered that there employment contracts for next year have been cancelled.

14. You seem awfully anxious to try and compare me with a king of the beach male sea lion. Tell me: do I really seem that territorial?

15. Since its apparent that the dockworkers are going to honor there committment not to cross the picket line, over twelve million board feet of lumber are going to stay on those ships.

16. The young coach feels badly that her highly-touted forward has not been setting the world on fire.

17. She has entitled her new work "Smart Like Me;" however, she says she's recieving considerable resistence from her publisher about it.

18. For the fifteenth time!, I didn't rob those stock certificates.

19. Donny's and Marie's new hit single lacks that exhilirating star quality punch.

20. Inflation is one of many evils which tends to perpetuate itself. For example midwestern farmers can't cope with fifteen per cent interest rates and those rates are fueled by banks attempts to attract new savers.

Name _____

Grade or score _____

# EXERCISE 28

# Clarity and conciseness

**Purpose**  To use grammatical skills to construct clear, concise sentences.

**Reference**  *WWC*, Chapter 8

**Instructions**  Without altering the meaning of the following sentences, rewrite them, paying particular attention to unnecessary words and phrases, awkward sentence construction, lack of parallelism or anything else that takes away from clear, concise expression. Write the clearest, most straightforward sentences you can.

1. It is a fact that the council meeting will be presided over by the mayor whose name is John Lively.

2. Plans for the senator's scheduled appearance in the city of Pine Valley are still being finalized as of this moment.

3. Journalists who don't pay attention to detail, people who work as reporters who do not prepare very well for interviews and the kind of reporter that can't seem to get a story in at the time when it's due are just the type of reporters that Barbara Wexler, a managing editor, really doesn't like too much.

4. Buying and restoring old antique furniture is a hobby Arthur Martinson truly loves, and now it has become the way that he makes his true living.

5. What the agency is attempting to try to do is to get people to work on the parking problem themselves.

6. Wondering when interest rates for mortgage loans will go down to something that's less than 12 percent is a concern on the part of those people in the Northwest who make their living off of the timber industry.

7. Despite the fact that at this point in time there is no reason why the senator should announce her plans, she went ahead and called a press conference anyway.

8. He won the award on account of the fact that his photograph was considered to be the most unique.

9. The consensus of opinion of the instructors was that to pass the test, a very solid background in Greek was needed.

10. Being surrounded by thirty journalists who are all famous, as well as all having won national awards, can make a person feel really humble.

11. Seeing as how a fatal accident caused the untimely death of two truckdrivers, new warning signs in regards to the dangerous S-curve are being installed by the highway crew.

12. Referring back to the original document, he repeated again his previous statement that he said before about how concerned he was that the wording was not very clear.

# Boiling 1

**EXERCISE 29**

**Purpose**  To eliminate wordiness and redundancy by editing a passage for maximum clarity.

**Reference**  *WWC*, Chapters 8 and 9

**Instructions**  Review the following account and rewrite it into a coherent story, *half as long as the original.* Put facts in a cohesive order, without losing any essentials. Follow AP style.

After he lost control of his late-model automobile when a butterfly flew into his face, Thomas Fitzpatrick, who is 38 years old and who lives at 2467 Tokay Lane, crashed into a large plate glass window of a Middletown supermarket this afternoon at about noon and completely destroyed two cash register stands, 35 grocery carts and a giant display of insect repellent spray cans.

Fitzpatrick, a plumber who works for the Chase Co., reportedly was not hurt, according to the police officers at the scene. But there was substantial damage to the E-Z Shop Market, which is located at 428 Hoover Avenue. Market manager Joe Albertson said he estimated the damage at around $30,000 after he made a preliminary estimate.

Fitzpatrick's car, a 1985 Audi Turbo, was totally demolished beyond repair. However, no supermarket patrons were injured, according to police reports.

In another accident across town, police reported today that Helen Demming's Corvette Stingray automobile hit a fire hydrant after she lost control of the vehicle. No one was injured, however, according to eyewitnesses.

Demming said that she took her hands from the steering wheel of the car (she was driving at the time) when she tried to slap at ants that were crawling around her ankles. The insects were "big and red," she said.

"I was really startled," said Demming. "You don't expect to find giant red ants in your car." The incident happened at 11 a.m. this morning. "The next thing I knew, my car smashed into this fire hydrant," said Demming, owner of the real estate brokerage of Demming & Walsh Co. "I guess I lost control."

Police said her car received only slight damage but that several businesses in the 400 block of Madison Ave. in Middletown (where the accident occurred) suffered flooding damage to their basements when storm sewers overflowed from the hydrant runoff. A damage estimate is not complete.

Demming is 29 years old. She lives at 1234 Burgundy Street. The crash happened at the corner of Madison and Polk Avenues.

(337 words)

Name _____

Grade or score _____

# Boiling 2

**EXERCISE 30**

**Purpose** To continue your editing practice on a passage that is wordy and redundant.

**Reference** *WWC*, Chapters 8 and 9

**Instructions** Review the following account and rewrite it into a coherent story, *half as long as the original.* Put the facts in a cohesive order, without losing any essentials. Use AP style.

What might have been nothing more than a minor traffic accident last night turned into an unfortunate tragedy when an out-of-control car sped into a group of people huddled at a bus stop and sent four women crashing through a plate glass window at 201 Cleveland Street.

Two of the women in the accident were killed, and another was critically injured with broken and severely cut legs. A fourth woman is at Municipal Hospital and is in satisfactory condition. There were no other injuries, according to police.

Police officers and witnesses said the accident occurred when a bright yellow car heading east on Cleveland Street struck the left side of a black convertible heading west on the same street. According to various reports, the yellow car went out of control and sped toward a group of 10 people waiting at a bus stop in front of Faunce Drug Store at 201 Cleveland. The car was halted by a 3-foot brick wall below the store window—but not until four women were struck by the car and were hurled through a large section of plate glass.

One of the victims, whose legs were almost severed, was pronounced dead on arrival at University Hospital. An investigation revealed that she was Alpha Bates, 78, of 311 McKinley St.

A second woman, a 75-year-old widow named Emma Smith of 235 Waubesa Avenue, died at Municipal Hospital 40 minutes after the tragic crash. A hospital representative said the woman's legs had been severed at the knees.

Next of kin have been notified in both deaths.

The injured women were reported to be 48-year-old Thelma Jones, who lives at 974 Mc-

Clean Street, and Betty Chafee, who is 27 years old, of San Francisco. Jones is listed in critical condition. Chafee is listed in satisfactory condition. Both women are in Municipal Hospital.

Police continue to investigate the accident. The driver of the car that struck the women apparently escaped from the scene, and police are following up on leads to track down the suspect.

Funeral arrangements are pending.

(345 words)

Name _____

Grade or score _____

# Leads 1

**EXERCISE 31**

**Purpose**  To practice clear, concise, grammatical sentence construction in the context of writing news leads.

**Reference**  *WWC*, all chapters, especially 3 and 8

**Instructions**  Carefully review each of the following sets of facts pertaining to news stories. For each set of facts, construct *one* clear, concise, grammatical lead sentence. Neither all the facts nor all the details should—or could possibly—be included in one sentence. In this exercise you are practicing news judgment as well as sentence construction.

## Story 1

- Dog killed by speeding automobile.
- Accident happened at 10th Ave. and Baker St.
- Accident happened 6:55 a.m.
- Seeing Eye dog belonged to Harry N. Beals, 10 S. Davis St.
- Beals unhurt.
- Driver of car did not stop.

## Story 2

- Two hunters, Martin Behrend and William Brown, both of Crowell.
- Driving an '81 Ford pickup on Interstate 5.
- An eagle attacked the vehicle; crashed through windshield.

- ☐ Happened 8 miles south of Urbanville this morning.
- ☐ Unhurt, the eagle clawed William Brown.
- ☐ Inflicted painful face wounds.
- ☐ Behrend stopped truck, used rifle butt to beat eagle until it flew out window.

## Story 3

- ☐ Sara F. Glasser is president of the local chapter of the American Civil Liberties Union.
- ☐ She announced a new membership drive today.
- ☐ Chapter usually solicits members by mail only.
- ☐ New membership drive will be made house-to-house starting next week.
- ☐ Glasser says ACLU chapter needs 50 new members.
- ☐ "The chapter needs to replace members who have moved away," she said.
- ☐ "If we cannot do so, we must disband the chapter," she said.

# Leads 2

**EXERCISE 32**

**Purpose** To continue practicing clear, concise, grammatical sentence construction while developing news judgment.

**Reference** *WWC*, all chapters, especially 3 and 8

**Instructions** These stories are presented in the form of a reporter's notes. Read the paragraphs carefully and extract the information you need to write *one* lead sentence for each story. Clarity, conciseness, grammar and style should be major considerations.

## Story 1

Big fight between the Urbanville Ambulance Squad and the Urbanville cops has been brewing all week. Police Chief Rod Ryan ordered his traffic control officers not to stop traffic at intersections to let the ambulances through. One cop (won't go on record with his name) said Ryan told officers to stop ambulances for speeding. The Squad, all volunteers, really angry. Felt cops were interfering with their work and complained to Mayor Helen Lund and the county board of commissioners. Last night, at a special executive session of the Board called by the mayor, Ryan resigned.

## Story 2

Budget committee meeting last night. City manager David Mardan presented his proposed budget, calling for expenditures of $88.2 million. This is $5.5 million more than the current budget. Mardan told the committee members he figures the revenue collections will be about $2.3 million short of the expenditures, even with all the budget cuts proposed by the committee and a special city task force that's been working on the budget for the past 3 months. Mardan said he doesn't see that any more cuts will be possible. He told the committee that taxes are going to have to be raised. Lots of discussion. Committee meets again next Thursday.

**Story 3**

Just got a call from University of Urbanville news bureau about a third-year medical student named Kenneth R. Nelson from Springfield, Massachusetts. He's going to bicycle from Boston to Seattle this summer, hooked up to all kinds of sophisticated, lightweight equipment that will measure heart rate, calorie consumption, skin temperature and a number of other things. It's part of a project designed to figure out how the human body adapts to intensive training. A van with two university researchers and a physician will keep pace with Nelson. Head of project is Dr. Clark Simpson, who chairs the sports medicine department.

Name _____

Grade or score _____

# EXERCISE 33

# Final grammar, spelling and word-use exam

**Purpose**   To evaluate your performance and progress with a comprehensive examination of grammatical principles.

**Reference**   *WWC* (all)

## PARTS OF SPEECH

**Instructions**   Identify the *underlined* part of speech.

_____ 1. Sheldon feels <u>bad</u> about the broken window.

   a. adverb   b. adjective   c. pronoun   d. gerund

_____ 2. It looks <u>as if</u> it's going to rain.

   a. preposition   b. adverb   c. conjunction   d. participle

_____ 3. She will head the <u>specially</u> commissioned panel.

   a. adverb   b. adjective   c. noun   d. verb

_____ 4. <u>Between</u> you and me, these ticket prices are getting out of hand.

   a. conjunction   b. preposition   c. adverb   d. verb

_____ 5. <u>Lifting</u> weights can give you more flexibility than you think.

   a. noun   b. adverb   c. verb   d. adjective

83

## IDENTIFICATION OF SENTENCE ELEMENTS

**Instructions**  Identify the *underlined* sentence element.

_____ 6. Do you really believe <u>that the sun will come out tomorrow</u>?

      a. independent clause
      b. dependent (subordinate) clause
      c. adverbial clause
      d. appositive phrase

_____ 7. <u>Running on concrete</u> isn't the best thing for one's knees.

      a. subject of sentence
      b. participial phrase
      c. introductory clause
      d. predicate nominative

_____ 8. <u>After the circus left town</u>, I realized I had spent my life's savings on the water balloon game.

      a. prepositional phrase
      b. independent clause
      c. appositive clause
      d. introductory subordinate clause

_____ 9. <u>Besieged by creditors</u>, the financier quickly left town.

      a. adverbial phrase
      b. participial phrase
      c. subordinate clause
      d. prepositional phrase

_____ 10. She decided to leave all her money <u>to the SCA</u> (Society for Creative Acronyms).

      a. appositive phrase
      b. prepositional phrase
      c. participial phrase
      d. adverbial clause

## SENTENCE TYPES

**Instructions**  Identify each of these sentences according to its type. Use the following code: a—simple; b—compound; c—complex; d—compound-complex; e—fragment.

_____ 11. Despite the ravages of a poor economy, this is going to be a good year for us contractors.

_____ 12. I thought this plan would work out, but I guess I was wrong.

_____ 13. Hitting the brakes for all he was worth as the vehicle sped wildly down the road.

_____ 14. The snowfall has clogged all the passes, but the daily newspaper still managed to get through.

_____ 15. Harmonicas that are made of plastic don't hold a tune very well.

## AGREEMENT, CASE AND PUNCTUATION

**Instructions**  Select the correct answer from the choices offered.

_____ 16. Beyond the horizon of an ordinary mind *(a) is (b) are* adventure and intrigue.

_____ 17. She is one of those politicians *(a) who (b) whom* party bosses never can accept.

_____ 18. There is no better graphic designer than *(a) he (b) him.*

_____ 19. Baseball is one of those games that *(a) require (b) requires* close attention to the rules.

_____ 20. Neither the attorneys nor the contractor *(a) has (b) have* been linked to the bidding scandal.

_____ 21. The Senate won't confirm his nomination *(a) because (b) , because* it doesn't feel he has the background to handle such a sensitive post.

_____ 22. This weather is the type that could really injure spring crops *(a) , however, (b) ; however (c) ; however,* a warm front should move in soon.

_____ 23. The *(a) witness' (b) witness's* story did not support the plaintiff's testimony.

_____ 24. Herschel is the kind of actor *(a) who (b) whom* moviegoers love to watch.

_____ 25. This award will go to *(a) whoever (b) whomever* receives the highest score on the Scholastic Aptitude Test.

_____ 26. A number of exceptional works of fiction *(a) has (b) have* appeared on the book market recently.

_____ 27. Finding and tackling "impossible" projects *(a) has (b) have* always stimulated Sarah to new levels of accomplishment.

_____ 28. More than 70,000 tons of relief supplies *(a) has (b) have* been airlifted to Ethiopia and Somalia.

_____ 29. Police arrested the demonstrators *(a) and (b) , and* took them to a high school gymnasium for fingerprinting and processing.

_____ 30. Are you going to see *(a) "Camelot?" (b) "Camelot"?*

_____ 31. Neither of the witnesses *(a) sound (b) sounds* very credible.

_____ 32. I know you're surprised, but the winnings in the Washington lottery are *(a) yours. (b) your's.*

_____ 33. Your criteria for evaluating my paper *(a) is (b) are* capricious.

_____ 34. None of the witnesses *(a) has (b) have* shown up for the Jackson trial.

_____ 35. It's going to be another *(a) rainy, Oregon winter. (b) rainy Oregon winter.*

## SPELLING

**Instructions**   Pick the *correct* spelling from the choices offered in the following sentences. Enter the appropriate letter in the blank on the left or on your answer sheet.

_____ 36. The wierd villain weilded a deplorible influence over the group.
          (a)         (b)           (c)

_____ 37. Can you be innoculated against the ravages of tonsilitis and pnuemonia?
                      (a)                      (b)          (c)           (d)

_____ 38. The playright was embarassed that she neglected to secure a copywright for her
              (a)              (b)                                        (c)
colossal new production.
(d)

_____ 39. The sherriff's appointment calender is barely manageable; he must learn to
              (a)                    (b)              (c)
withold more of his time.
(d)

_____ 40. In all liklihood, his was a concious effort to destroy the concensus of the amiable
                (a)                (b)                          (c)            (d)
group.

_____ 41. What do you mean, "His judgment is infalible"? That's a decietful arguement.
                                (a)          (b)              (c)        (d)

_____ 42. The physicains hypothesized that massive doses of caffeine contributed to his
              (a)                                          (b)
horrable hemorhage.
(c)       (d)

_____ 43. It's presumtuous of you to assume that this is a plausible occurence. It's
              (a)                                        (b)         (c)
a deploriable act.
(d)

_____ 44. The sargeant ordered everyone to remain stationery. She said she didn't want
              (a)                                (b)
to hear the rusttle of a single piece of khaki.
            (c)                          (d)

_____ 45. This predicament stupifies me. I'll need perserverance and incorruptable conduct
                            (a)                    (b)              (c)
to resolve this dilemma.
                (d)

## WORD USE

**Instructions**   Select the correct answer from the choices offered.

_____ 46. Let's drive *(a) farther (b) further* down the road.

_____ 47. He didn't mean to *(a) imply (b) infer* in his speech that you are dishonest.

_____ 48. Mussolini's corpse *(a) hanged (b) hung* in the town square.

_____ 49. This dietary plan is *(a) composed of (b) comprised of* four nutritionally approved stages.

_____ 50. You really seem *(a) anxious (b) eager* to do this.

_____ 51. It's beginning to look *(a) as if (b) like* the grand jury will return an indictment.

_____ 52. Contract negotiations have broken down *(a) among (b) between* Smith of the American League White Sox, the National's Cubs management team and free agent Winfield.

_____ 53. *(a) Compared to (b) Compared with* last year's inflation rate, this year's increase is hardly noticeable.

_____ 54. What *(a) affect (b) effect* do you think this grading policy will have on us students?

_____ 55. The club could not approve your membership in its Royal Order of Obfuscators *(a) because (b) since* you write too clearly and logically.

## IDENTIFICATION OF GRAMMATICAL ERRORS

**Instructions** Read the following sentences and determine whether they contain grammatical errors. If a sentence contains an error, select the lettered item that describes the error. If the sentence is correct, select *e, no error.*

_____ 56. Please buckle up your seat belts as soon as you get in the car, it's the best way to protect yourselves.

    a. *It's* should be *Its.*
    b. Comma should be replaced with semicolon.
    c. *Buckle up* is awkward and redundant.
    d. Both b and c are correct.
    e. No error.

_____ 57. The argument which I was going to pursue in my closing statement has proved itself a winner in several product liability cases.

    a. *Product liability* should be hyphenated as a compound modifier.
    b. *Proved* should be replaced with *proven.*
    c. Subordinate clause should be set off with commas.
    d. *Which* should be replaced with *that.*
    e. No error.

_____ 58. The man whom police arrested for the crime has an airtight alibi; however, police are not willing to drop the charges.

    a. *Whom* should be replaced with *who.*
    b. Improper punctuation has created a comma splice.
    c. Error in subject-verb agreement.
    d. *Whom* should be replaced with *that.*
    e. No error.

_____ 59. None of the stockholders are going to press for a proxy battle, but they certainly showed the board they can mount a well-organized campaign.

    a. No hyphen needed in *well-organized*.
    b. Error in subject-verb agreement.
    c. Semicolon needed before *but*.
    d. Pronoun *that* needed before *board* and *they*.
    e. No error.

_____ 60. Working with all his might to trim the mainsail, the wind abeam fought his every move; but he finally brought his craft under control.

    a. Coordinating conjunction requires only a comma before it.
    b. Dangling participial phrase.
    c. Semicolon needed after *mainsail*.
    d. Two sentences required for clarity's sake.
    e. No error.